To Lily,

Inheritance

poems

KERRY-LEE POWELL

All my thoughts
are with you at this
time. With great thanks

inheritance

poems

KERRY-LEE POWELL

BIBLIOASIS
Windsor, ON

FIRST EDITION

Library and Archives Canada Cataloguing in Publication

Powell, Kerry-Lee, author
    Inheritance / Kerry-Lee Powell.

Poems.
Issued in print and electronic formats.
ISBN 978-1-927428-79-5 (pbk.).--ISBN 978-1-927428-80-1 (ebook)

    I. Title.

PS8631.O8373I54 2014   C811'.6   C2014-903806-2
                                            C2014-903807-0

 Canada Council Conseil des Arts
for the Arts du Canada

 Canadian Patrimoine
Heritage canadien

 ONTARIO ARTS COUNCIL
CONSEIL DES ARTS DE L'ONTARIO
50 YEARS OF ONTARIO GOVERNMENT SUPPORT OF THE ARTS
50 ANS DE SOUTIEN DU GOUVERNEMENT DE L'ONTARIO AUX ARTS

Biblioasis acknowledges the ongoing financial support of the Government of Canada through the Canada Council for the Arts, Canadian Heritage, the Canada Book Fund; and the Government of Ontario through the Ontario Arts Council and the Ontario Media Development Corporation.

Edited by Zachariah Wells
Typeset, designed and copy-edited by Kate Hargreaves

PRINTED AND BOUND IN CANADA

CONTENTS

i.

Inheritance	11
Seals	12
The Emperor	13
Perdita	14
The Encounter	15
Big Spender	16
To My Creditors	17
Jig	18
The Other Grandmother	19
The Last of the Hitlers	20
Song for a Sleeping Father	21
Respite	22
The Wreckage	23
Ship's Biscuit	24
Fallowfield Station	25
The Lifeboat	26
Hellespont	27

ii.

Whiskey Mantra	31
Fandango	32
Skinnydipping	33
Silver Devils	35
Muskrat	36
Two Views of a Stag	37
Malefic	38
Curse of the Magdalene	40
Bachelorette	41
Get With Child a Mandrake Root	45
Inhuman	46
The Rich	47

Russian Brides   48
The Girls Who Work
  at the Makeup Counter   50
Tenderfoot   51
Lore   52
Family Jewel   53
Bernadette   55
Florilegia   56

iii.
In the Halls of My Fathers   59
Negative Theology   65
Grand Mal   66
Wilted Lotus Flowers
  at the Former Summer Palace   67
Ghost Lake   68
Hensol   69
Mirror Lake   71
Tantum Ergo   73
The Answers   75

For Andrew—with love and squalor.

INHERITANCE

Your winter coat, frayed at the wrists.
A cassette of your voice reciting verse.
A fear of King Lear. A belief in ghosts.

SEALS

Five humps on a rock: seals
basking in the same gust
that buffets my hat across the shale.
A hundred yards of cold froth,

lichen and moss lie between us.
From this distance their skulls
seem human, the luckless heads
of plumbers or night custodians

abandoned by loved ones,
limbs pilfered mid-nap,
packed away with the lunch things
as a mythical prank.

A lunge for my hat disturbs them,
the mottled faces abruptly turn.
What is it that approaches,
with its flailing hair, its dangling bones?

THE EMPEROR

His bent antenna hooked it
and like a legendary fish
it hauled us to the shoulder
so we could be submerged by it.

Beethoven's Emperor, my old man and I,
crammed into his last great wreck.
Windows taped shut, the ice holes
carved in the windshield

slowly misting over with our breath.
The notes came high and icily
then deepened into thunderheads,
filling the car with cut glass

that crackled into the static
of another radio station's maniacs.
He reeled the dial back in
and my father, now twenty years dead,

conducted the piano and the lead violin.
His bony finger arcing overhead,
he leans to me across the leatherette.
This is how you do it, he says.

PERDITA

The stones are poised mid-air
like an arch or a Japanese garden,
each in its own speechless, stunning moment,

strung up in the clouds like notes in an aria,
now suddenly face-sized, notched into angry masks.
The darkening sky is cathedral-thick,

the hull of the whole hard world
grinds me to the bone, breaks me like sticks.

THE ENCOUNTER

An old man on a folding lawn chair,
his bald head and freckled hands
reflected in the ornamental pond

with its tadpoles and its muck
and the whirring of the pump
he has spent all day trying to fix.

He pokes it with a stick,
stirs the ink, muttering to himself
and to that muttering lunatic

who gazes back up as a lifetime
of clouds and debris flit across his face,
mesmerized and wavering.

Not the dark overlord
he imagined in his youth,
whose eyes spiraled like drains,

but more a grim buddy
smirking at him in green-flecked slacks
from his cave beneath the lilies.

BIG SPENDER

As a shoal of goldfish scatters,
or a wet dog shakes diamonds,
coins flew from him in all directions,

into the caskets of buskers,
the sequined laps of dancers,
and the Styrofoam cups of beggars.

To the moons of Jupiter,
to the coffers of the sun,
how his coppers and his silvers spun!

When spent, he liked to imagine
them gathered like a Chinese dragon,
a fireworks suspended in mid-air:

all his riches hanging there.

TO MY CREDITORS

A dozen red razors.
Eleven peals of manic laughter,
ten impending crises.

Nine duels at dawn followed
by eight candlelight vigils.
Seven sighs, six lies, five

excellent excuses.
Four of my firstborns
—three of them bastards—

two brinks of despair,
one portent of disaster.
And O, the moon you asked for.

JIG

With the smirk of a girl
not scrubbed from my gob
I swung hard with the oafs
strewed my years like pods,

spread my smock
on the rutted field,
spun stars in a giddy fog.

Now light as a sprig,
I swig dregs from the jug,
and I rattle my gourd
with a scoured mug.

THE OTHER GRANDMOTHER

The flame-haired one who spat words like lava.
Flung them like clods of earth or whatever else
came to hand. Frying pans, pots of soapy water.
She knew a weakling when she saw one,

sized it, like a leopard from her baobab,
the kid with chicken legs or sensitive skin.
No sooner had one more arrived than the others
learned to walk upright and make weapons.

They fled in droves, filling the ship-holds,
inventing steam engines. They joined the circus.
They scaled mountains. They swam
the English Channel slathered in beef tallow.

All to be rid of the other grandmother,
tits down to her ankles, eyes like hot stones.
It was no use: she was in high dudgeon.
She was everywhere they were, like the family chin.

Fanning her embers, nursing her grudges.

THE LAST OF THE HITLERS

The storm tore a pier off Long Island Sound,
unearthed a row of oaks and a Mafioso corpse
from the grounds of the Federal Reserve.

New York at dusk is neo-classical,
all columns and wingless silhouettes
crowding the high windows.

Down here it's sewage and hazard warnings,
sirens shrieking like bereaved women
and the last of the Hitlers on his daily walk,

holding the frail vial of his body taut
because he's vowed to spare the world his blood
and let the ignominious line die out.

If he spills a drop the taint will spread,
infect the causeway and the flooded marsh.
Last of the Hitlers, last of the Patriarchs.

Although in this gloom he could be you or anyone,
a Canute who seeks to command
the engulfing waves with a stay of his hand,

while a fresh storm on the Atlantic gathers force.
Let the Greats smash
their pianos in resounding finales,

lash the air with salt and applause
for this lone man at the land's drowned end,
as if he was the last monster, the last god.

SONG FOR A SLEEPING FATHER

Animals spoke in the worlds he created.
He liked to lose himself beside me in those places,
away from his bed, his heart full of holes,
his kingdom of cold spaces.

They sink their teeth into me later—
Shadow-rat, Claw-pig, and the Dark Horsie.
I crawl from these dreams to his room on all fours,
and beg him to make them disappear forever.

He knows the magic spell, my sleeping father.

RESPITE

Caught in the lamp's amber,
the man whose wrung hands
hang limp at his sides,
having scourged the air and more,
and the hurt elsewhere,
a child asleep upstairs.
Above the rooftops, massed
clouds darken like bruises.

THE WRECKAGE

If all is wrecked between us, it's because
a pair of wing tips on the other side of the world
closed in prayer to make this small breath,
like the breath of a child blowing a candle-wish,

that only gathered salt and squalls as it grew swift.
They say it often begins like this.
The ends of the earth are littered with our fragments
like flocks of terns on an arctic ice-cliff

or words on torn-up sheets of paper
in a language that I try not to remember,
spelled out again like moths around the flicker
of your face that often flares at me in strangers.

Look how I make the most of what's at hand,
a match-girl out for kindling, in a windy land.

SHIP'S BISCUIT

After mother scarpered
it was ship's biscuit
with shrapnel sparkles.

It was hot spurts and gristle
and cold snaps with a wet towel
for stealing a puff from dad's fag

or sneaking a peek at his titty mags.
But we buggers deserved no better.
It was us that made her run off,

with our bickers and our bungles.
It was our bloody cheek.
It was his bleeding knuckles.

FALLOWFIELD STATION

The night train spills its inkblots into the ether.
The bundled shapes fog the air,
hump bags towards a fluorescent bunker.

I peer through the glass past my own ghost
into a hushed sea of suburban
houses without souls, or so I imagine.

Who's to say they're not lined with mother-of-pearl,
and filled with their own soft murmurings?

THE LIFEBOAT

All night in his lifeboat my father sang
to keep the voices of the other men
who cried in the wreckage from reaching him,

he sang what he knew of the requiem,
of the hit parade and the bits of hymns,
he sang until he would never sing again,

scalding his raw throat with sea water
until his ribs heaved, until the salt
wept from his eyes on dry land,

flecked at his lips in his squalling rages,
streaked the sheets in his night sweats
as night after night the reassembled ship

scattered its parts on the shore of his bed,
and the lifeboat eased him out again
to drown each night among singing men.

HELLESPONT

after Anselm Kiefer

When everywhere is where the light was
and the foreshore dissolves in the roiling dark,
each wave is an uprising, an outbreak of war
and darkness is the crest, darkness the trough,
and nowhere is the haven he must swim towards,
when everywhere is where the light was.

Kursk, Thermopylae, Troy, Kharkov.
Ypres, Salamis, Cannae, Somme.
Gravid with shrapnel and shed blood,
the sea grows darker with each onslaught.
A million faces in a million waves are lost
when everywhere is where the light was.

As a sprung leak sinks a barge,
the evening news unreeling, every mass
grave, every black grain in the seen footage
immerses him in boundless dark,
when everywhere is where the light was,
and nowhere is the haven that he swims towards.

WHISKEY MANTRA

I went through the whiskey,
I passed through the fire.
All faces blurred.

The half-moons under my eyes
engraved themselves in the mirror.
Until broke, I drank the silver.

I went through the whiskey,
I passed through the fire,
became a thief, a mendicant, and a liar.

I raged, I swore.
I contemplated becoming a whore,
all for the world

to spin each night around my bed
while I saw stars.

I went through the whiskey
I passed through the fire,
I dream all night about tigers,

about glass after glass of water.
I wake up with this thirst, this fear.

FANDANGO

The hen-nighters set him off but didn't notice,
the epileptic in the red suit.
It wasn't the strobe or the mirror ball
but the camera-flash blue
lighting up the dance floor like an August storm.
And the bride-to-be, the bride-to-be
dragging her tin cans, her veil
of condoms and IUDs, her heavy head
reeling between snaps. Then later,
the developed set: a hundred flailing red
flashes of his arms, his many tongues, his legs.

SKINNYDIPPING

The campfire's sunk to a ruin.
Let it glow from a distance

like Rome or Atlanta.
Abandon all pretense

at keys, clothes, loose change
and the world falls to your ankles.

Hang the last vestiges on a branch
to bear fruit or witness, but be fast,

too long a pause at the water's edge
might turn you to salt or a Narcissus,

so slip. Let the hard cares of air
and land collide and dissolve,

the owl in its bower of needles,
fretworks of pine and fern,

the drawn blade of a new moon,
subdued in the ripples. Regress—

to the knee, the waist, the neck.
And having lost yourself,

why not most that's human—
all claims to the throne,

crime scenes and danger zones.
Cut the blood-ties and drift,

an algae bloom, a phantom limb.
A cloud of unknowns,

without harm. Without origin
or end.

SILVER DEVILS

For Monica and Cherie on their wedding day

You say we're too alike, as if it were a crime.
If true, then technically we're felons.
As frauds of each other, we should do time
together. Upon reflection,

far worse is to falsely imitate,
at least a mimic is no liar
and what could be more natural than to ape?
Even stars must sometimes admire

their own imposters in the lake,
and look how heron delves into heron
to filch a glint of silver in its beak.
We'll feast forever, kin upon kin,

I, your replica and you, my counterfeit,
for mirror faced with mirror, equals infinite.

MUSKRAT

You spy it in the roadside murk.
Cat, you say. Or maybe dog.
A blur of fur as the car speeds on.
A trick of the dusk. A hunched knot
undoing itself in the sprawling dark.
Something else you thought,
you saw vanish in the rushes, or not.

TWO VIEWS OF A STAG

King of the backwoods
photo-op. Carved
into chops. Zip-locked.
A stack of red chunks
hauled in a pickup
to a hick's chest freezer.

Snapped on crags. Bagged
in gouache, Victorian oils,
mounted on plaques.
An ingress of bone unfurled
above a burled walnut
executive desk.

Heart's snagged wound.
Horned god of the room.

MALEFIC

What isn't clear is how she keeps breathing
in the locked trunk of his car, mouth and nostrils

taped or how he steers the slack heap
of her body up the stairwell to the unlit

place he often dozes in while shady figures
on the screen steal off with other bundled shapes

in loosely strung narratives but where also he lies rapt
staring up through cracked plaster

to where his secret star throbs like an ache
in the temples, spelling out the nightly pattern

and pace of the recurring thoughts that spur him
to become at first a dimly felt presence

between streetlights and entrances
but every now and then a face, blurring amid

stunned winces and repeated blows in the unkempt
room that shifts in and out of focus,

ink spraying in all directions, because she
is a bird in a chimney

fingers smeared with soot, reaching for her one
chance of escape, when the grabbed fabric

drags behind her in that ordeal from the window
to the bathroom where he is a looming angel

to whom she falls in sudden worship, across slicked
tiles and into fragments in black plastic,

back in the trunk and again when the officials
dredging the canal look up to guess which high rail

he has leaned from, the unknown perpetrator
to see his own ill-defined silhouette in the water

and the weighted sack shatter that brief mirror.

CURSE OF THE MAGDALENE

Slung like a sack of cats out of every bar.
Stripped to the waist like a witch in the village square.
Stoned. Star-struck. Kissed.
Kissed on the mouth by God's gift.
Show-off. Bitch.

BACHELORETTE

Armaggedon

Lights flash from the wizard box.
Somewhere in the night club
a sound like glass doves

rises and cascades back down on us.
Our arms revolve like windmills.
This is serious.

A Little Latin

Stomping the cha-cha in platform shoes.
Downing Bellinis, rubbing razor burns.
Fux and Reflux.
After that, I don't remember much.

The Ladies' Room is Always Haunted

The door blows in a background chorus.
Toilets flush, one after the other.
Heels on tiles make tap dances,
a virtuoso plays the hand drier,
against the disembodied voices.
Sometimes it sounds like a musical,
chopping up lines in your cubicle.

Never Fall Asleep with the Radio On

I dream I'm born again in country music.
The first wail knocks me cold and gets me Christian.
star-crossed as Wile E. Coyote always rising

intact from my canyon, brushing off rubble and flies,
taking my explosives to the barn dance
lining up sinners into a terracotta army

bursting like buckets and pots into fine red pieces,
the colours and textures of a spaghetti western.
I drive off in my truck. To Tucson. With the music on.

If it was up to me I never would have chosen this.
But Jesus H. Christ, what a banjo riff.

GET WITH CHILD A MANDRAKE ROOT

You come turbo-charged.
Blood beats through the blades in your heart
like a tanker, spilling your dark
in a sea of bed lit up by LCD only.

Just the thought gets me off
in another dimension, then I'm free,
like an animal, on the savannah,
in Africa, on TV.

Let children play with aerosols and loose sparks.
Let pets explode in microwaves and all parks
make way for future development.
Let stars war on Astroturf. Do I give a fuck?

We've got physics! We've got chemistry!

INHUMAN

They called from the hospital to say
this time you were really dying.
I was fifteen, late home from the movies,
mouth bruised from kissing.

I'd seen so many deaths on the screen,
with knives and guns, capes and fangs.
Death didn't drain off into an armchair
as monotonous as your laboured rasp.

Twice I stood by you, shifting from one
leg to the other, my kindnesses stolen
from soaps, from stars with skin like milk,
their breasts over the flattened soldiers.

At the hospital I couldn't pretend
I wanted to lean into you as the others leaned
to heave their grief out into kisses. I backed off,
tried to look like a loved one, a human.

It's no wonder that your face
visits my face in the mirror the least often.
My neglected grandfather, I would like you to have seen
that string of teenage suck-marks around my neck.

Your blood, my first romance.

THE RICH

Our mamas hauled
ass in their rusty Novas,
chugged breakfast colas,
shone rich folks' silver,
buffed the ballroom
parquet like jilted belles.

At the back of the Empire
arcade, knees on the cold
linoleum, in the shade
of the stadium's
terraces, in the bucket
seats of their Audis,

we daughters blew the rich
boys hard, as if
our lives depended on it.
Chins slicked with spit,
blew them like fat chances,
like the luck we never had.

RUSSIAN BRIDES

Feast on spoils from oil
barons. Are feral cats,
fake as implants. Thrive on air

and vodka. Have been trained
from day one to show the least
emotion, are as inhuman

as Olympic gymnasts
or double agents.
Skilled as Bolshoi swans

their wild cruel charms
are like martial arts or Kamikaze,
luring icons and stars

from cliff-tops to the sharp
bleak rocks in their slanted
Slavic hearts.

And they are coming,
in spiked heels, with sunken
cheeks, they'll stop at nothing.

Like the new nouveau riche,
or the old ex-Soviet elite
grasping at silks and jewellery.

They're stealing millionaires!
They're scaling buildings!
Like that girl with the fairy-tale hair,

not Rapunzel but the one
snapped up among one-eyed
bumpkins in a defunct hamlet

by talent scouts in Siberia,
and groomed for super-stardom.
She did *Vogue*, she did *Cosmo*.

She let it all down one early
Sunday morning, a twisting rope
of honey gold, a hundred stories.

The long, slender body
smashed but still miraculously
sheathed in its evening gown.

THE GIRLS WHO WORK AT THE MAKEUP COUNTER

The girls who work at the makeup counter
live holy lives, and drink each hour
seven glasses of rainwater.

The girls who work at the makeup counter
live holy lives, and sleep in herbal blankets
each night for fragrant hours.

The girls who work at the makeup counter
live holy lives, and wake to paint
one sunrise on each eye.

TENDERFOOT

You knew the reservoir was for drowning,
but you went in up to the waist, plunged
for your lost change and any other twinkle
that you never recovered. You knew the noon
train might blast in from a sudden
silent nowhere and take your head off
but you laid your last coin on the rail,
choked on tar and dust until it thundered past.
You knew the fires in the vacant lots
might turn you to ashes, but you heaped
the chairs you took from the church hall
watched the smoke twist into hooks
and wondered, who will be king?
You were told the air after bedtime was off-limits
but you fled into that forbidden emptiness,
the skyline a snare of flashlights, closing in.

LORE

His old mam scrubbed slabs, slung
pails of grey froth across the cobbles
while his dad chipped flint in the drowned
quarries, downed bitter at the Lamb
and Flag while all the kids
waded up to their shins, built crude dams
out of stones plucked from the icy river,
then knocked them down again
and again before supper, because that's
how it was back then, each day a chink
between a wash of dark and wind.

FAMILY JEWEL

The opal ring I stole
from a friend's jewellery box
overflowing with gifts
from aunts and older cousins,

of which there were so many,
and such an abundance
of gift-giving ceremonies.
Any saint's day was an excuse

to drape her neck in gold
or anchor each finger to a precious stone.
Sticky with candy and dirt, it lay tucked
all day in my shorts, cutting a ruby wedge

into my private parts. Even buried
at home in a basement chest
it caused an itch, not quite of guilt
as it lay nestled amongst the cast-off stuff,

but a kind of atheistic urge
to find a use for it beyond my kneelings.
Or was it malice, or was it love
that made me bring it up, a snake's egg

in a twist of cloth, to place
in my father's palm and claim

it was found like a silverfish
under a rock? To him it meant

a trip to the pawn shop and relief
from some pressing want.
Nothing good could come of it,
that milky eye lidded

with an iridescent murk.
But how could I foretell
that the man appraising the ring
was an uncle and his niece's loss

already spoken of,
or that my father's frown
meant I would never be forgiven
for that walk, bare-handed

through the knowing town.

BERNADETTE

Of all the things she left behind,
the strapless and the floaty numbers

the slinky tubes with unhooked collars
and her a loose woman

sharing herself with God knows
how many others,

of the string bikinis and unlaced corsets,
rolled into flimsy balls and flung

by my thunderous father
to the bottom of the cellar steps,

clinging to rough plaster,
strewn in musty floral drifts,

the star of the entire moldering mess
was her sheer floor-length nightdress.

Snagged on a nail by the furnace door,
ballooning with each warm blast,

a familiar haunt as the years passed,
the nylon sparkles catching

what little light there was.
Queen of all underthings,

a shower of pink gauze,
our unholy phantom, lady love.

FLORILEGIA

Spring

When the moon is a blade
in a meadow of stars
stay curled in your bud
like the wish that you are.

Summer

Who cares if we're broke as a drunk
pair of rubs on a park bender?
The roses are pink as a starlet's pout,
the trees are billionaires!

Fall

A blaze of leaves in a sky of ashes.
Witches once lived here. And fanatics.

Winter

The front yards are full of frauds:
a coal-eyed battalion with twigs for arms.
At first light, with our picks and shovels,
we'll build an ice palace. We'll make angels.

IN THE HALLS OF MY FATHERS

There are no exits, only entrances and hallways,
windows overlooking fountains and peacocks,
their blue iridescence like dusk on the quadrangles.
There is the music of distant muskets, footsteps on polished
marble, and rooms, rooms, rooms adjoined by portrait galleries
where the faces of dukes bump against the varnish
like carp in an aquarium.

God-lit. Dimmed by Germanic gloom,
sunk beneath an amber craquelure, the world
immured year after year in oils, in tempera,
mounted in glazed mosaics the seigneurial eye
gloats upon as it would a new wife's curves.

Save me Beethoven. Save me Plato.
Come God, come echoing Hereafter,
let the Greats swagger on the horizon.
Whistling girl, crowing hen:
graced and effaced by dead men.

He has buried his ship with him.
Every wave, every glint his eyes saw
is sunk with him like a Viking's hoard.

He has buried his ship with him,
now he sails the unseen world,
cleaves the earth's dark seams.

He has buried his ship with him,
his hull like a husk of the seed
from which new ships have sprung.

He has buried his ship with him,
the way a miner stakes his claim,
massing a trove of unearthed gleams.

And now all ships belong to him,
every seen fleet, every ghost
of a glimpse on the sea's sheen.

An ancestral mask hangs in my hallway.
Rubbed too much for rain or luck,
the braille of its carved cheekbones

is wearing off, like St. Peter's bronze
foot in the grand basilica. Like the tin
man from Oz, it longs to be human,

not faced with the same front door
and temporal variations:
flakes of alchemist's gold,

then the bare calligraphy of winter branches.
Let this swathe of veils
regale all hollows with droplets and ghosts

that lift and sink as if to music.

In a cave lit by torches
in a kingdom that never was,
in irons and in battle-dress,
in mournful Greek choruses
down infinitely receding corridors,
from bulwark and palisade,
from the depths of my bellicose
heart: one by one, none by none,
my old fathers calling forth.
In a cave lit by torches.
In a kingdom that never was.

NEGATIVE THEOLOGY

She wanted to get away from yes,
the horns and traffic, but mostly fingers
burrowing beneath her twill capris
frisking buttocks, filching wallet and ID.

Tearful scenes at the embassy
couldn't restore her to her former self
and so she walked among the numberless
with neither name nor fixed address,

fair game to any Roman with a roving hand.
How she kept an open mind
was anybody's guess, viewing the bones
of Capuchins in the overcrowded

crypt. But this is how it happens:
sickened by the oglings and stiffs,
the head cranes above a mass of other heads,
sees null eternity and welcomes it.

GRAND MAL

The Lord of Fumes is gnawing the Trevi fountain,
pitting the cheeks of Oceanus, pocketing the small
valuables of tourists. Smokes black the travertine
of my two-star hotel, scribble futurist manifestoes.
Il Duce's motorcades nose into the new era.

WILTED LOTUS FLOWERS AT THE FORMER SUMMER PALACE

The royals may be wintering in hills, gloating at spoils,
calling from the deeps of village wells. Of these details the lotuses
in the photograph do not tell. They are a note scrawled in haste
the wilted seed pods like blotched ink against the mist's pallor,

mistakes replicated in the lake's mirror. A hostage's botched escape.
What chance did they have in any case, when the eye behind the lens
has caught even the palace's slow dissolve into white?

GHOST LAKE

The former residents of the drowned village
returned by the busload to see their steeple
emerge in a dry spell from the hydroelectric
reservoir's diminished waters. On calm days
the remains of the old hall's walled garden,
greenly wavering. Year after year they came,
spreading blankets on the embankment.
like the shed leaves from the surrounding birches,
the water's shifting mirrors caught their looks of sad
enchantment, as if figures in a recurring dream,
gliding off in boats over lilac stumps and the cellars
of demolished houses. Wistful flotillas,
how their faces lit up momentarily then fell
because it was hard to tell whose swamped yard
had been whose. Sometimes they wished
they could dive to the bottom and drift
among the ruins to find the shining thing
they looked for, but never found.

HENSOL

For David and Martin John (1968-2009)

It's winter. The condos are behind schedule: the artist's
impression hangs from the billboard in tatters, the sketched greenery
spattered with snow and dump-truck slush and a nebulous
FUCK sprayed in red aerosol, the K trailing off in sympathy
for all that remains unfinished. To keep warm, the workers
have sheathed the window holes and outer structure
in semi-opaque plastic, so that I see only a crude smear of faces
peering out on smoke breaks at the surrounding blur,
and then again the empty window spaces, like dark patches
in a frozen river. It's not that I'm complaining, it couldn't remain
a vacant lot forever. But it had a kind of Zen perfection,
the few quiet boulders reflected in shallow pools after rain
and the late blaze of goldenrod in the depression
where a row of long-demolished houses had been.
The condos will draw new blood in from the suburbs,
the balconies will be hung with wreaths and coloured bulbs
and each room filled like a glass with wavering light.

At night it's a white palace. It's a ghost ship trapped in ice,
overrun with gusts: the crackle of plastic, tarps and snapping ropes
assault my dreaming ear like the cold, clairvoyant music
of a Russian composer in the early twentieth century,
unleashing a tirade of terrors that has me writhing in my sleep
or up parting my curtains in a mute panic.

It's like the beginning of the end of my marriage,
the day we threatened but hadn't quite begun to re-enact
the chilly traumas of our childhoods on each other.
Too stunned to stay home, we swigged from a shared flask,
wandered until our heels ached, stepping at last through a culvert

onto the grounds of the abandoned sanatorium. It was so long ago,
an almost make-believe land, seen through scrolling trees,
the boarded-up, castellated hall, rusting gates and brambles.
Rhododendrons glowed like coral brains in the undergrowth,
the ruins of a vanished garden. As if in a different realm,
white shapes in terry-cloth robes flitted on a distant lawn:
the members of an adjoining spa pretending not to notice
as we trespassed along the weedy path then craned to look
through the slats and barricades into the gloomy lower rooms,
strewn with metal chairs and falling plaster. And I saw them
as clearly as if they were figures in an old documentary,
the men with minds of children, moving in slow groups
from the dining hall to the outer villas, unearthing rows of onions.
Basking on warm benches, wrapped in hospital blankets,
marvelling from barred windows. Heading back
into semi-darkness, and in all the years that have followed since
I thought it was a miracle such a place existed, that we had fallen
by chance into a rare state of grace, and learned nothing.

MIRROR LAKE

All weekend the outboard engine
has been failing, unspooling rainbows

on the lake's surface, slicking the fingers
of the drowned aspen, whose wheel of upturned

roots seems like the emblem of an ancient
cult of death, or nature, or both.

High on the ridge, the tents are collapsing.
It's the end of the season, and the last families

gather at the taps to rinse battered pots,
undo the squalor of fire pits and laundry,

their children streaked in calamine and soot.
On the other side of the lake, spires of smoke

loosen into smog. Through the trees
a stream of leave-takings, Windstars

and Dodge Caravans, their cargo of faces lost
beneath the canopy of sky and branches

that flickers on the windscreens past
the carved mascots flanking the exit.

In winter the snow-swept cabins
will have the look of an abandoned village,

the cedar planks exhaling resins
into the half-buried interiors.

A hundred miles to the north
they've unearthed a Wendat city,

its tubers spread beneath a Toronto suburb:
longhouses, palisades and a gallery

of cornhusk effigies rotted to lace,
a rusted European axe head at the exact centre,

lodged like an ache in the cerebrum.
A gust perturbs the water's face,

the gunwales tilt and shudder.
We're also in the middle of something,

terse words and a stalling engine.
Tinged with blood and amber from the fallen

leaves, the run-off of centuries,
our semblances tremble in the waves.

TANTUM ERGO

They're tearing down the church on Dominion
and St. George. The pastor in his bulletin
cited shrinking parish, higher costs.

Now a crowd stands by the barricade,
watches the wrecking machine
smack a chunk of buttress into loose bricks.

My neighbour in the post-war bungalow
used to mow the churchyard while his wife
dusted the sacristy with lemon Pledge.

They've come out to the end of their drive
to see the belfry slump, then an empty sky
clouded with fine particulates.

It sounds like pack ice busting in a swell,
windows and girders and cement lintels
cracking and buckling in the dozer's claw.

A breach in the wall and the exposed nave,
its inner gloom, the upward yearning of vaulted oak
is unreal against the ruptured mortar seams

like a painting by an old master
overlain on the mouth of a cave. Another shove
splinters the arthritic wood,

the pitched roof sags, as though in shame.
The wrecking crew steps back, intent
as hunters circling big game.

Seconds later it's a mound
of shingles and burst sticks. What will be
built in its place, someone asks,

barely heard above the shifting debris.
The foreman cups his ear, responds
with hands upturned, eyebrows raised.

THE ANSWERS

Tell the king, the fair-wrought house has fallen. No shelter has Apollo, nor sacred laurel leaves; the fountains now are silent; the voice is stilled.
    Last prophecy of the Oracle at Delphi

Athens vanishes in a blast of dust. I spent my last night
there with an ex-marine, crowned king of the Phoenix
monster truck circuit, both of us drunk and seeking
oblivion, because the Parthenon was closed for repairs
and the streets stank of garbage and death.
There are whole suburbs in Florida
choked with mournful beauty, their abandoned pools
filling slowly with rain. The Greek hills are strewn
with the half-built villas of luck's has-beens,
their poured foundations at a distance
indistinguishable from ancient ruins. My Phoenix
king's snake-handling Baptist forefathers
have blessed him with vacant eyes and a mistrust
of philosophy. But he knows trauma, blunt
or otherwise, has no beginning, no end,
only knots and kinks around which the mind
bends and groans, the remembered explosions
blooming beneath closed eyes again and again.
From our bus the Aegean is a mass of gleams,
the bleached walls in the villages
blank as the pages of an unwritten book.
We're a time machine, a dented silver capsule
speeding up Mount Parnassus to the Delphic
Oracle with a tour guide in epaulets and fake military
regalia. Bruised, crosshatched with scars,
my Arizonan twitches at each thrust of the bus's engine

then slips back into fitful sleep. He has come to Greece,
like me, to find an explanation for his own heroics,
the way an abandoned child might seek a father
among the relics and unearthed torsos,
but has found so far only sunstroke and Retsina.
I can feel them as we walk the path from parking lot
to ruins: the questions, spoken or etched
on tablets, crushed underfoot like mollusk shells
into fine dust over the millennia.
Our guide tells us about Delphi's glories,
Plutarch's treatise on rust and how through
the mouth of a writhing woman, the Oracle spoke
to anyone who climbed the temple steps with wrung hands,
in tongues and grandiose language,
in beauty and anger and unbearable tenderness,
whose eyes turned inward and tunnelled down the wartorn,
blood-soaked centuries, past the blooming of countless
explosions, to see us staring back, indifferent as ghosts
on the steps to the crumbling stadium, the guide pausing
by an empty pedestal where Apollo's
statue once stood, the passengers disappearing
with cameras over the rock face, snapping fragments
of a moment that they may or may not linger over in years
to come, recalling the smell of pines and diesel,

the silver capsule speeding its way back
to Athens, through groves and along the coast,
and the answers, glancing off rooftops,
striking the cliff face, abrading the rocks.

ACKNOWLEDGMENTS

Poems in this collection have appeared in *Ambit Magazine, CNQ: Canadian Notes and Queries, CV2, MAGMA Poetry, Poetry Wales, The Spectator, Riddle Fence, Sampler Magazine, The Malahat Review, The Winnipeg Review,* and *The New Quarterly*. A version of this manuscript was awarded the 2013 Alfred G. Bailey Prize by the Writers Federation of New Brunswick. "The Lifeboat" and "The Emperor" won *The New Quarterly'*s Nick Blatchford Occasional Verse Contest and were subsequently nominated for a 2011 National Magazine Award. "Hensol" was nominated for a CBC Literary Award and "The Wreckage," originally published as "Sonnet," was nominated for a Pushcart Prize. Sections of "Bachelorette" appeared in *Pterodactyl's Wing*, an anthology of Welsh poetry edited by Richard Gwyn.

"Hellespont" was inspired by Anselm Kiefer's Velimir Chlebnikov series. "Hensol" is the name of a former mental hospital and private mansion in Wales. "Get With Child a Mandrake Root" borrows its title from John Donne's song "Go and Catch a Falling Star."

I am grateful to the Canada Council for the Arts, The Arts Council of New Brunswick, The Banff Centre for the Arts, and to the Jeanne and Peter Lougheed Endowment Fund for their financial assistance.

Heartfelt thanks to my editor Zach Wells for his patience, wit and acuity, as well as to Dan Wells, Tara Murphy, Kate Hargreaves, Chris Andrechek, Jesse Eckerlin, John Metcalf and everyone at Biblioasis. I am indebted to those who have read and graciously commented on versions of this manuscript: Anthony Howell and Pamela Stewart, Karen Solie, Jen Hadfield, and Daljit Nagra, and to writing group friends Beth Janzen, Allan Cooper, Lee Thompson, Carol Steel, Elizabeth Blanchard, Danny Jacobs and Andre Touchburn. Thanks also to friends from Wales who influenced some poems in their earliest incarnations: Samantha Wynne-Rhydderch, Cecilia Rossi, Robert Minhinnick, Richard Gwyn, Gwyneth Lewis and David Greenslade. I'm grateful to Kim Jernigan, Pamela Mulloy and John Barton for first publishing this newcomer in Canada, to Ross Leckie and Gerard Beirne for welcoming me to New Brunswick, and to Jeffery Donaldson for his wonderful reading of "The Lifeboat" at The Jeweller's Eye.

Love and gratitude to Arthur Leonoff, Lana Coe, David and Marlene Powell, Gareth and Brenda Powell, Glyn Maxwell, Gary and Gail Buzzell, Monica Carter, Cherie Sturm, Gerhard Becker and all my other friends and family for your humour, generosity and light, and for taking in this stray when she needed a haven.

To my late father Meurig Powell, who suffered terribly and still tried, alone and in great hardship, to raise his two children.

And thanks most of all to my brother Gareth, for being there and still being here.

ANDREW BUZZELL

Born in Montreal, **KERRY-LEE POWELL** has lived in Australia, Antigua, and the United Kingdom, where she studied Medieval and Renaissance literature at Cardiff University and directed a literature promotion agency. Her work has appeared in journals and anthologies throughout the United Kingdom and North America, including *The Spectator, The Boston Review,* and *The Virago Writing Women* series. In 2013, she won *The Boston Review* fiction contest, *The Malahat Review*'s Far Horizons Award for short fiction, and the Alfred G. Bailey Prize. A chapbook entitled *The Wreckage* has recently been published in England by Grey Suit Editions. A novel and short fiction collection are forthcoming from HarperCollins. *Inheritance* is her first book.